Going Places

Jill Malcolm

Notes for the Grown-ups

This wordless book allows for a rich shared reading experience for children who do not yet know how to read words or who are beginning to learn. Children can look at the pages to gather information from what they see, and they can suggest text to tell the story.

To extend this reading experience, do one or more of the following:

Ask children to share about the types of transportation they have experienced.

Introduce vocabulary such as these words when looking at the pictures and telling the story you see:

- airplane
- bicycle
- bus
- car
- feet

- go
- move
- scooter
- skateboard
- stroller

- subway
- transportation
- tricycle
- van
- walk

Discuss how the types of transportation change as a person gets older. Talk about how these and other types of transportation can be used at various ages.

After reading the pictures, come back to the book again and again. Rereading is an excellent tool for building literacy skills.

Have children sort types of transportation into categories, such as air, land, and water.

Consultant

Cynthia Malo, M.A.Ed.

Publishing Credits

Rachelle Cracchiolo, M.S.Ed., *Publisher*
Emily R. Smith, M.A.Ed., *SVP of Content Development*
Véronique Bos, *VP of Creative*
Dona Herweck Rice, *Senior Content Manager*
Jill Malcolm, *Graphic Designer*

Image Credits: all images from iStock and/or Shutterstock

Library of Congress Cataloging in Publication Control Number:
2024013625

Teacher Created Materials

5482 Argosy Avenue
Huntington Beach, CA 92649
www.tcmpub.com
ISBN 979-8-7659-6142-1
© 2025 Teacher Created Materials, Inc.
Printed by: 926. Printed In: Malaysia. PO#: PO11723